Flipping Leadership Doesn't Mean Reinventing the Wheel

Peter M. DeWitt

CORWIN
A SAGE Company

CORWIN
A SAGE Company

FOR INFORMATION:

Corwin

A SAGE Company

2455 Teller Road

Thousand Oaks, California 91320

(800) 233-9936

www.corwin.com

SAGE Publications Ltd.

1 Oliver's Yard

55 City Road

London EC1Y 1SP

United Kingdom

SAGE Publications India Pvt. Ltd.

B 1/I 1 Mohan Cooperative Industrial Area

Mathura Road, New Delhi 110 044

India

SAGE Publications Asia-Pacific Pte. Ltd.

3 Church Street

#10-04 Samsung Hub

Singapore 049483

Printed in the United States of America

A catalog record of this book is available from the Library of Congress.

ISBN 978-1-4833-1760-1

This book is printed on acid-free paper.

Executive Editor: Arnis Burvikovs

Associate Editor: Ariel Price

Production Editor: Amy Schroller

Copy Editor: Janet Ford

Typesetter: C&M Digitals (P) Ltd.

Proofreader: Dennis W. Webb

Cover and Interior Design: Janet Kiesel

Marketing Manager: Lisa Lysne

Certified Chain of Custody
Promoting Sustainable Forestry
www.sfiprogram.org
SFI-01268

SFI label applies to text stock

14 15 16 17 18 10 9 8 7 6 5 4 3 2 1

Flipping Leadership Doesn't Mean Reinventing the Wheel

CORWIN CONNECTED EDUCATORS SERIES

Teaching the iStudent: A Quick Guide to Using Mobile Devices and
    Social Media in the K–12 Classroom
By Mark Barnes @markbarnes19

Connected Leadership: It's Just a Click Away
By Spike Cook @DrSpikeCook

All Hands on Deck: Tools for Connecting Educators, Parents, and Communities
By Brad Currie @bradmcurrie

Missing Voices of EdTech Conversations
By Rafranz Davis @RafranzDavis

Flipping Leadership Doesn't Mean Reinventing the Wheel
By Peter M. DeWitt @PeterMDeWitt

The Edcamp Model: Powering Up Professional Learning
By the Edcamp Foundation @EdcampUSA

Empowered Schools, Empowered Students: Creating Connected
    and Invested Learners
By Pernille Ripp @pernilleripp

The Power of Branding: Telling Your School's Story
By Tony Sinanis @TonySinanis and Joseph Sanfelippo @Joesanfelippofc

The Relevant Educator: How Connectedness Empowers Learning
By Tom Whitby @tomwhitby and Steven W. Anderson @web20classroom

Contents

Preface

Welcome to the Connected Educators Series.

The past few years have provided momentous changes for educators: Whether it's the implementation of the Common Core State Standards, educational innovations due to technology, teacher and administrator evaluations, or budget cuts, what is clear is that educational reforms come in different shapes and sizes. For many connected educators, one of the invaluable group support systems essential during these times is the professional learning network, also known as our PLN.

Our PLN can provide innovative ideas, current resources, and sound educational practices that stretch our thinking in ways we haven't yet experienced. Equally as important as how a PLN can professionally expand our horizons, it introduces new friends that we look forward to meeting in person. This Connected Educator Series brings together some important members of my PLN. These are educators with a depth of knowledge and level of experience that helps me stay current and up-to-date with my educational practices.

In this series, my book, *Flipping Leadership Doesn't Mean Reinventing the Wheel*, takes the innovative idea of flipping classrooms and presents it at the school leader level, engaging the school community in new and innovative ways. In *Connected Leadership*, Spike Cook shares his experiences moving from a novice to digital leadership and illustrates how other educators can do the same.

Digital experts Steven Anderson and Tom Whitby help increase your digital experience by using Twitter to locate a PLN to engage in daily professional development. In *The Relevant Educator*, Tom and Steve provide a plethora of tools to use, and define each and every one. Using those same tools, in their book *The Power of Branding*, Tony Sinanis and Joe Sanfelippo help you to brand your school in order to create a positive focus on the learning happening within the four walls. In his book *All Hands on Deck*, Brad Currie offers us ways to engage with families and students using old techniques with new innovative approaches.

In *Teaching the iStudent*, Mark Barnes provides insight into the life and mind of the iStudent, and in *Empowered Schools, Empowered Students*, Pernille Ripp focuses on em**power**ing students and teachers. Also in the series, in *Diversity and Connected Learning*, Rafranz Davis shows how equity and diversity is vital to the social media movement, and why that is so important to education as we move forward.

Kristen Swanson from the Edcamp Foundation not only focuses on why the Edcamp model is a new innovative way to provide excellent professional development, but also explains how you can create an edcamp in your school district in *The Edcamp Model: Powering Up Professional Learning*.

The books in the Connected Educator Series are designed to read in any order, and each provides information on the tools that will keep us current in the digital age. We also look forward to continuing the series with more books from experts on connectedness.

As Michael Fullan has said for many years, technology is not the right driver, good pedagogy is. The books in this connected series focus on practices that lead to good pedagogy in our digital age. To assist readers in their connected experience, we created the Corwin Connected Educators companion website (www.corwin.com/con nectededucator) where readers can connect with the authors and find resources to help further their experience. It is our hope and intent to meet you where you are in your digital journey and elevate you as educators to the next level.

Peter M. DeWitt, Ed.D. @PeterMDeWitt

Acknowledgments

I am thankful for being on a team with Ariel Price and Arnis Burvikovs. Their experience, feedback, and collaboration brought this book series to life.

In addition, I would like to thank Mike Soules (Corwin President) and Lisa Shaw (Executive Director of Editorial and Professional Learning) for their support on this Connected Educator Series.

Special thanks to my partner Doug and my family.

Thanks to the Connected Educator authors. We all came from different places, and came together to show what is great about social media and professional learning networks. You all are awesome.

Lastly, thanks to Jim Hoffman, the Averill Park Central School District Superintendent (my boss), for his support as I took my leave of absence and ultimately resigned from my position as principal to follow a different path.

DEDICATION

To the Poestenkill Elementary School students, staff, and parents. All of you made the idea of flipping leadership come to fruition; without you, this never would have been a successful experience. I am honored to have been your principal for eight years.

PUBLISHER'S ACKNOWLEDGMENTS

Corwin wishes to thank the following reviewers for their editorial insight and guidance:

Thomas Hansen, PhD, Independent Consultant
Chicago, IL

Nicole Kemp, Principal
Williamsburg Elementary
Williamsburg, MO

Susan Kessler, Executive Principal
Hunters Lane High School
Nashville, TN

Angela M. Mosley, Assistant Principal
Armstrong High School
Richmond, VA

John Robinson, High School Principal
Newton-Conover City Schools
Newton, NC

Kathryn Wagner-West, Teacher/Administrative Intern
Robert Gray Middle School
Portland, OR

About the Author

Peter M. DeWitt (EdD) was a principal in Upstate New York since 2006. He is now an independent consultant focusing on school climate, connected leadership, and Visible Learning (Hattie, 2009), working with school districts, state education departments, and educational organizations nationally and internationally. Before becoming a principal, he taught elementary school for eleven years. His syndicated blog *Finding Common Ground* is published by *Education Week,* and he is a freelance writer for *Vanguard Magazine.*

Peter has presented at state and national conferences around the United States, including the National Association of Elementary School Principals (NAESP) Conference in 2012 and 2013 and the Association of Supervision and Curriculum Development (ASCD) Conference. His presentations focus on struggling learners, and educational technology, as well as safeguarding lesbian, gay, bisexual, and transgender (LGBT) students and other social justice topics. Peter is a regular commentator on the BAM! Radio Network where he discusses leadership and educational issues. (BAM! is an acronym for "body and mind," and BAM! Radio was conceived in 2007 on the premise that the key to success in life for children and youth is nurturing a healthy mind in a healthy body.)

Peter completed his doctoral dissertation on the subject of safeguarding LGBT students at Sage College of Albany in Albany, New

York. His book *Dignity for All: Safeguarding LGBT Students* was published by Corwin in March of 2012. He is a consulting editor and visionary for the Connected Educator Series (Corwin, Fall 2014). In addition to *Flipping Leadership Doesn't Mean Reinventing the Wheel* (Corwin, Connected Educator Series), Peter's forthcoming release is *Climate Change: How Do I Foster a More Inclusive School Climate* (ASCD, Fall 2014).

His articles have appeared in education journals at the state, national, and international level. He has written for *Principal Magazine, Education Week, Educational Leadership, The Huffington Post, ASCD Whole Child, Connected Principals, Smartblogs,* PBS, and *ASCD Express.* Additionally, he has been interviewed by the American Association of School Administrators (AASA), the National Education Association (NEA), the Association of Supervision and Curriculum Development (ASCD), Public Broadcasting Service (PBS), and ABCnews.com.

Introduction

Educators as well as school leaders are very busy and have to meet mandates and accountability measures at the same time as they negotiate their way through a more connected learning environment. Time constraints and initiative fatigue are seen as some of the barriers to new learning, so instead of piling one more thing on an already full plate, this book looks at innovative ways to shift our thinking, and refocus the ways we communicate with one another.

That is what is meant by the term flipped leadership. One example of flipped leadership is about making faculty meeting discussions more authentic. To that end, information is sent out ahead of time so teachers can prepare before a discussion takes place, with the result that everyone can go deeper with their learning.

The technique of flipped leadership can be used for any building or district level meeting, but just as important, it can be used to communicate with parents. In a time when parents want to know what they are paying for, as they cart their children from one activity to the next, flipped leadership allows leaders to give their parents a window into the world of their children. It helps promote school events, highlight special visits, but can also give a view into a day in the life of their child. For parents who cannot make it to school often, it gives them a topic to discuss with their children at dinner, but it also helps them understand that school has changed from when they were students. In a way, it makes school visible to parents, and it helps engage them in the school community.

As a school principal, I initially used flipped leadership on a whim because I saw the benefits of the flipped classroom. I hoped teachers would embrace it, and after a bit of work they did, but I had no idea that the day I took a risk and flipped my communication to parents that this was an idea to help build stronger communication between our school and parent community. I'm profoundly happy that I took the opportunity to flip my leadership. I hope that this book inspires you to take a risk, flip your leadership, and experience the exciting results.

LEARNING INTENTIONS

By the end of this book you will

- understand what it means to be a connected leader,
- understand the meaning of flipped leadership,
- develop an understanding of why connected education is so important to our flat world,
- understand the importance of flipping your leadership,
- learn how to flip your faculty meetings and parent communication, and
- learn how to make learning visible (Hattie, 2009) to the school community through flipped leadership.

"Old School" Leadership Communication

- Sending out monthly newsletters to parents, which is one-sided communication that tells them what we want them to know about school.
- Scheduling one open house at the beginning of the year where we tell parents what our expectations are for their children . . . and of them.
- Establishing a one page faculty agenda filled with a checklist of items that range from district initiatives to important dates for the faculty meeting. A meeting that usually ends with all parties heading in different directions, both logistically and philosophically.

- Relaying one size fits all e-mails to staff outlining the rules, what needs to change, and how to change it.

- Performing classroom visits that focus on what the teacher is doing, and not what the students are learning.

- Expecting students to be quiet in the hallway, and enforcing compliance among students and staff.

- Being the dean of discipline. Finding yourself at risk of always being reactive to events that take place in school.

- Focusing on monologue—a characteristic of old school leadership . . . instead of finding ways to engage in dialogue.

Connected Leadership

- Understanding that important educational topics can come up more often than at one faculty meeting per month.

- Sending out articles or inspiring blogs before a faculty or grade level meeting so everyone can discuss the information when they get together.

- Moving beyond surface-level information to always questioning whether we went deep enough with our discussions.

- Developing building goals that focus on collaboration and innovation, not compliance and rule following.

- Engaging in educational discussions every day of the year using different mediums of communication.

- Modeling the proper use of technology to students and teachers.

- Drawing evidence-based observations using a tablet, which not only reduces the time it takes to complete an observation by half, but symbolizes to students and staff that adults use technology too.

- Performing classroom visits that focus on student engagement in school, and also student learning.

- Engaging families by using technology in a variety of innovative ways.

- Flipping the educational conversation on its head so that all stakeholders feel as though they have a place at the table.

- Taking pictures of students learning, creating a five minute video, and sending it home to parents.

- Recording a video that focuses on new initiatives like the Common Core State Standards, and sending it home to parents a few days before Open House so they can come to school with questions.

- Sending report cards home a few days before parent-teacher conferences so they can digest the information and come prepared with questions.

- Making all stakeholders feel welcome at the same time we make learning visible to all of them.

- Understanding that our professional and personal lives thrive on connections.

- Building a professional learning network at the same time as we build a personal learning network.

- Using technology tools to be proactive in your leadership practices in order to spend less time being reactive.

That is where flipped leadership enters the leadership paradigm.

Connected Learning

The Precursor to Flipped Leadership

As a connected leader, and as someone who flipped his leadership two years ago, I find value in using technology. Nevertheless the avenues that opened due to those connections have completely changed the way I lead. Don't get me wrong, with the flipped approach, connected leaders have a good understanding of the pitfalls to avoid at the same time they try to push the envelope when it comes to using technology as a tool in the learning process. This wasn't a philosophy that I always held, but it was something that evolved as I became more open and resilient. It is fair to say that in the past I didn't always use all of the advantages of technology, which is why I didn't see the value in it, but some events in my life changed my perspective.

I taught elementary school for eleven years, mostly in a few city schools. One of those schools, Arthur S. May School, is located about 90 minutes outside of New York City. When I was first hired by Mr. May, it was actually called Arlington Elementary School, one of about six elementary schools in the Arlington Central School District. The school district was composed of an eclectic mix of parents living in poverty, blue collar workers who worked in Poughkeepsie, white collar workers who commuted to New York City on Metro North (the train), and a few professors from Vassar College and Marist College, which were both located a few minutes away.

Back in the 1990s when I began teaching, we did not have computers in our classrooms, and I didn't have one at home. E-mail communication existed, but a majority of the population didn't use it. I actually remember getting my first e-mail account in 1997. Although I don't use the account anymore, I still keep it as a reminder of my early days with technology. Is it really possible to be emotionally attached to an e-mail account?

To think about it now it seems crazy, but I used to type all of my papers during my graduate degree at Marist on the computer in the library at Arlington Elementary School. My last year at Arlington, we received computers. Unfortunately, due to my cluelessness on how to use them with students, those first computers were mostly used for keeping first graders busy by having them play games. I told myself it was a good *"brain break"* during center-based instruction, until the computers wouldn't work while I was trying to teach reading. A dysfunctional computer mixed with a group of first graders is a deadly combination. Believe it or not, I assumed computers were a passing fad. Yes, I was one of those teachers.

I moved on to another city school called Watervliet Elementary School, which is located just outside of Albany, New York. At that time I was on a committee that wrote and subsequently won a Reading First grant, a national initiative to improve reading in Kindergarten through Grade three. From ten days out of the classroom to writing grants—and almost one million dollars later—we received the grant and it changed the way we operated at Watervliet Elementary School. Some of the money went to buying new Dell computers for each classroom. It was quite the upgrade for our poor city school with a high percentage of students on the free or reduced lunch program. Most of the students did not have a computer at home, and my personal home computer was a Gateway, which was useful for cruising the Internet, and checking e-mail from a few computer-savvy friends. However, the previous philosophy regarding students' computer use at Arthur S. May School remained true at Watervliet. The computers were used to keep students busy during center-based instruction; only this time, I was able to secure some reading games, which seemed to work well with students. I'm not much of a gamer, but the games reminded me of playing Donkey Kong on Nintendo, only geared toward reading. As we all know, computers are out of date about a month after purchase, and we kept those Dell computers long past their typical lifespan. All of which made me seriously question the relevancy of computers in the classroom and the inequities between schools that did not have them and those schools that did.

● ● ● ● REFLECTION

Did you grow up in a time before computers were commonplace? What are your earliest memories of utilizing technology? What was your first computer?

SHIFT HAPPENS

I served as the Principal of Poestenkill School in Upstate New York and worked with teachers who used technology flawlessly, and others who were afraid of it. We were fortunate in our rural/suburban school district because we had an outstanding technology director, and correspondingly, a superintendent who valued technology. Working together, they built an infrastructure that brought Smartboards to every elementary school classroom. Combine this with a visionary assistant superintendent who valued distance learning, and the team created a distance learning lab in the high school.

Over time, I saw an explosion of handheld games, tablets, and then smartphones introduced into the schools. To the students, this wasn't the introduction of some foreign technology, it was a natural part of their lives. When we noticed that handheld games were quietly slipped into the school, some teachers and aides wanted them banned, which is a common reaction of many schools. Teachers and school leaders like to ban technology and social networking sites because they can't control them, and then they blame the students and their parents for the downfall of all humanity. Statements are made, such as *When I was a kid I used to go outside,* or *these kids play too many video games,* all of which is mixing issues. It is possible to remain connected and still find the balance to disconnect from time to time.

During this period, my own thinking began to shift, and instead of banning handheld games, I encouraged students in the fourth and fifth grades to use them during inside recess. In one of my first flipped experiences, I sent the staff an article about banning handhelds, and then met with them at our support staff meeting to discuss the idea of embracing the technology, instead of banning it. It is impossible to send students outside in below 20 degrees weather, so I thought this was a better alternative to banning and could provide us with the opportunity to teach students how to use their handheld games when it was appropriate in school.

On reflection, that was when my flipped leadership experience really began. I provided information ahead of time to the staff so that when we were together we could explore more deeply our understanding of the subject at hand. Instead of banning handhelds, I flipped our old rules on their head, and took the time to engage students in the dialogue of learning how to appropriately use technology, instead of the continuing the ineffective monologue of demanding adherence to rules that focus on why something is not allowed in school.

As my flipped leadership evolved, and the pressure of completing evidence-based observations increased, I bought an iPad to use to complete observations, because when you're in a brick building on 27 acres of land in a rural area, connecting to the Internet is spotty at best. I was able to use the Pages application on my iPad, and created a Danielson cheat sheet, which I could then e-mail to my office after completing the observation. (The Danielson form is an observation and evaluation form commonly used to develop schoolwide or districtwide reports.) I could then take the form and cut and paste it into the district-approved form used for postobservation conversations. The information was completely transparent, and the teachers always received all of the notes taken during the observation. Using my iPad and the Pages app cut the time required for the observations in half, and helped make the actual postobservation conversations more valuable; now my focus was on learning, and not just completing the task. As an example, it was typical for my administration colleagues to take four hours to complete an observation, whereas my observations usually took less than two hours. At the same time as some of them dreaded the process, I looked forward to it, because I flipped my emphasis from getting it done, to really focusing on student engagement. There was also an indirect benefit. I was modeling the use of technology to our students and teacher colleagues. Professionally, technology enhanced my leadership experience.

Too often educators are resistant to technology, and yet the reality is that they have always been surrounded by innovative technology, such as television, radios, and many other devices. Teachers often cite the negative byproducts of using technology, such as cyberbullying that happens to our students or when the Internet goes down during power outages—both of which are issues—but they don't justify throwing technology out the window. We can't *"throw the baby out with the bathwater."* Instead of banning forms of technology, we should model the behavior we want to see. Banning is an issue all schools should address. After all, how many educators try to ban technology at the same time as they carry their own smartphones into school? We, as educators, have a real opportunity to teach children how to use technology in an ethical way and to focus on appropriate behaviors, instead of any bad habits they may discover on their own.

●●● CONNECTED MOMENT ●●●

- How do you feel about banning technology? Does your school have a ban? Why?

- Do you believe that teachers and school leaders have the power to teach students how to use technology in acceptable ways?

SETTING THE STAGE
TO FLIPPED LEADERSHIP

A couple of weeks after I began writing my *Finding Common Ground* blog for *Education Week*'s online magazine, I joined Twitter (an online social networking and microblogging service that enables users to send and read short 140-character text messages, called "tweets"). I really didn't see the use in it. It's hard to see the use in something when you have no followers and aren't sure who to follow. After a couple of weeks, I stopped using my account. I signed off and tuned out. It was two years before the Cairo situation with my brother, and it wasn't an earth-shattering decision because I hardly had followers. I decided to give it a second chance, and rejoined about one month later. Twitter didn't send me a card for rejoining or anything, and I still wasn't sure there would be any benefits, but on one random Saturday afternoon in September as I was sitting on my couch, I encountered a chat session. I noticed everyone talking about elementary education using a hashtag (a word or phrase preceded by the symbol # that classifies or categorizes the accompanying text) called #elemchat. Within five minutes, I joined the conversation and was hooked. I could not believe that in 140 characters I could participate in dialogue about education. After a couple of months of participating in #elemchat, I wrote the following blog.

Why Educators Should Join Twitter

In late July, I decided to join Twitter. To be perfectly honest with you, I had no idea what I was supposed to do when I got on there, but I heard so much about it I thought it would be a worthwhile experience. The only concern was that we have so many distractions already in life that I wasn't sure that I needed to add one more to the list.

I consider myself fairly technological, and given the amount of time I spend checking e-mail, I know that I am "connected." I have a smartphone, iPod, iPad, and laptop, and I created my own website. For a long time I thought Twitter was a venue for celebrities to tweet their every move, so it wasn't anything that interested me, but I figured I would give it a try.

Lynn, the director of technology in the school district where I am a principal, kept telling me that Twitter is great because it streamlines the information you receive. She is a "techie," knows about all of the latest 21st century tools, and I trust her judgment. Also, I did like the idea that Twitter offered "one stop shopping" for all of my educational needs.

Too many times in the 24–7 media, we are hit with images we would rather not see. As I get older, I have less of a need to hear most of the news on the television. Lynn assured me that with Twitter, you choose to follow people with your common interests so that when they tweet information, you are exposed to articles, blogs, videos, quotations, and

(Continued)

(Continued)

information that you find valuable and relatable. She certainly made it sound interesting.

Every month I made new connections, but I wasn't really into the whole experience. Then, in early September something amazing happened. I actually understood what Twitter was all about. All of Lynn's advice came rushing at me when I found an elementary education chat session happening on a Saturday afternoon. I have to admit that I wasn't sure what #elemchat meant, but I saw a few of the people I was following add that phrase to what they were posting. I decided to click on #elemchat, and I found educators from all over the world posting advice and resources for elementary education.

That was the moment I became hooked on Twitter. Connecting with people from around the world who have similar interests and understand your passion for education is inspiring. Although educators get accused of accepting the status quo and not wanting to move forward, Twitter is a place where that accusation is proven wrong. Educators who do not know each other and have never met, and may never meet, share their best practices, wisdom, or advice.

We live in the 21st century where our students don't just "*do*" social networking; it is a part of who they are as digital citizens. To many educators, it's a big deal to get on Facebook or Twitter, whereas to our students, it is something they cannot fathom living without. Understanding their connection with those sites increases an educator's connection with their students. The ability to talk a student's language may even provide an opportunity to break through to that hard-to-reach student.

Unfortunately, many educators know students that are hard to reach. Sometimes an educators may feel less comfortable reaching out to immediate colleagues and more comfortable reaching out to people on Twitter that they follow or who follow them. Many times those Twitter colleagues can provide really valuable resources to help educators meet the needs of these inaccessible students.

In addition, there are millions of people on Twitter, including organizations with great resources on such issues as homelessness, bullying, special education, and gifted education. Socially and emotionally numerous students are dealing with issues that many educators never had to deal with, and a social network like Twitter and its member organizations can help educators assist their students and parents by connecting them with many valuable resources.

Professional Development

Many educators are intrinsically motivated to find their own professional development. They read websites and blogs and are members of organizations that send them journals. They read more educational materials than they read books for fun. Twitter is one resource they should add to their list because they will discover blogs, articles, and videos that they probably would never be exposed to on their own. There is just too much information in cyberspace to locate all of these resources using regular search engines.

Many schools no longer have a great deal of money to pay for professional development, which is unfortunate because those experiences can be very educational. The budgets that those school districts do have are often earmarked for the best possible professional opportunities that tie into district goals.

Another value with Twitter is the professional development aspect where educators ask for help from their followers and the people they follow. Those questions are quickly answered, and resources are often provided as well. Other times when visiting Twitter, educators find conversations and read thought-provoking quotations and blogs on topics that may generate a new interest for them.

Connecting with colleagues from all over the world who have similar interests is really amazing. As much as any of us may believe that our

(Continued)

(Continued)

> Although conferences and one-day trainings are always beneficial if educators put into it what they get out of it, Twitter offers daily professional development in the privacy of your own home.

present circumstances are difficult, which they may be, connecting with educators in other countries helps to put things into perspective. Sometimes the situation for those educators is much harder than ours is and they need our help, and other times there are educators who are in schools that inspire us and provide a worthwhile goal to work toward.

The following are some suggestions regarding establishing and using a Twitter account:

- Although there are privacy settings, be careful what you write.
- Remember that everything you post can be made public.
- Keep it respectful, as if your students or your grandmother were reading your post.
- Make certain you watch the amount of time you spend on Twitter: it is easy for hours to pass by quickly.
- Don't forget to check in with your loved ones every once in a while!
- Twitter should never supplant professional development, but it can supplement it, particularly during difficult financial times.

In the End

Connecting with like-minded educators from around the world helps lift us out of our present situations and allows us to aspire to specific goals, even if some of these resources teach us how to live creatively within our parameters. Those compatible educators can also help us meet the needs of our students. Once we have exhausted all of our other known resources that are within close proximity, Twitter can provide us with resources that we never knew existed.

Our students enter our classrooms coming from diverse backgrounds and exposed to diverse experiences. Some of those experiences may be helpful to their development, while other experiences may be detrimental to their development. All of that diversity often makes it hard to meet the needs of each and every student.

Although Twitter cannot solve all of the problems of our students, it can provide educators with ways to help those students. In addition, it may help inspire educators to try new things in their classrooms. Who knows, it may even create a relationship where educators and their students can connect with other educators and students from across the globe and open up new experiences for everyone involved.

....

Source: http://blogs.edweek.org/edweek/finding_common_ground/2011/11/why_educators_should_join_twitter.html

Establishing a Twitter account became a precursor to flipping my leadership process. All of these moments are interconnected. Twitter opened me up to social networking, which helped me create my Professional Learning Network (PLN). A PLN consists of people who frequently respond to you, or ask for assistance. They are educators, researchers, and parents who you trust, and have educational conversations with, regardless of whether they always agree with your thoughts. Using Twitter helped me connect with research about the flipped classroom, which I then gave to my teachers. Twitter was also a place where someone challenged me to flip a faculty meeting, which led to flipping my parent communication.

It was easier to establish a PLN because I was on Twitter every day and, by virtue of my responses, established a back and forth communication with a number of people. Over time, people began to follow me and I followed in return. We engaged in discussions, and followed up with e-mail, Google Hang Outs (GHO) (Google+ Hangouts is a messaging app that lets you send and receive messages, photos and videos, and even start free video calls, one-on-one or with a group) or Skype sessions. The PLNs in the virtual world work the same way as in our real world.

As I bonded more and more with educators from around the world, the more new experiences I was introduced to and the more my world became flat. Over time, I found other chats, and began adding the words *"Connect with Peter"* at the end of my blog. Not only were people reading the blog, but they followed up with me to provide their thoughts on what I wrote. It opened up a dialogue around numerous educational topics. It was through those chats and other discussions on Twitter that I found my voice; a funny thing happened on the way to Twitter, I feared technology less.

A little over three years later, I look forward to the times when I am sharing with my PLN. We have met at state and national conferences, organized an edcamp, and connected through GHO and Skype. We have become friends who talk on the phone, and share ideas through Twitter, e-mail, and other methods of communication. We have supported each other through hard times and provided strength to move forward with new initiatives. That is what a PLN does. In the words of John Hattie (2012), they become your *"Impact Partner."* An impact partner is someone who provides effective feedback to you and helps change your practices.

WHO NEEDS A PLN?

The simple answer is that every leader needs a PLN. Leadership is challenging because we have to work with personnel, children, and the public, and depending on the day this can be the greatest part of the job, or the worst. Having a PLN allows leaders to go outside of their school district to find confidants to help them whatever the issue. Having a third party who is not always a part of our day-to-day lives is important because he or she has an outside perspective that may help us discover our best thinking.

It's not just the people within a building that can make life hard from time to time. Other administrative colleagues sometimes help create negative circumstances as well. Especially those colleagues who are resistant to technology and social networking. Typically, there are a few leaders in a district who are tech-savvy, and a high quality PLN can help support leaders who feel as though they are going it alone. The bottom line is that a great PLN supports you when you need it, challenges you when you least expect it, often stretches your thinking, and provides friendship when you need it the most. We get out of a PLN what we put into it.

ACTION STEPS

- Create a Twitter account.
- Begin following people you respect.
  - Examples:
    - Todd Whitaker @ToddWhitaker
    - Eric Sheninger @NHHS_Principal
    - Tom Whitby @tomwhitby
    - Andy Hargreaves @HargreavesBC
    - Diane Ravitch @DianeRavitch
    - Steven W. Anderson @web20classroom
    - Begin creating a PLN.
- Find other school leaders whom you know are on Twitter.
  - Twitter offers suggestions based on the information you provided. Follow some of those educators, and they will most likely follow you back.
  - Tweet out to them. Some educators get an account and follow their feed without contributing to a conversation. You won't get much out of the experience if you don't participate.

- Join a chat session.
  - Google search Jerry Cybraryman. He has the most comprehensive list of chats on Twitter. I recommend #edchat on Tuesdays and #satchat on Saturday mornings.

DISCUSSION QUESTIONS

1. What does connected learning mean to you?
2. What are the negative aspects to social media?
3. What are the positive aspects to social media?
4. What is a PLN?
5. Why are PLN's important to leadership practices?

Is Flipping a Passing Fad?

WHY FLIP?

A few years ago, Jon Bergmann and Aaron Sams wrote a book called *Flip Your Classroom: Reach Every Student in Every Class Every Day* (Bergmann & Sams, 2012). Although some educators supported the idea and said they were using similar methods to engage students, it really was the first time most educators heard about flipped learning. Unfortunately, there were some naysayers out there who downplayed the idea and looked at the proposal as a way to get rid of teachers and replace them with online learning. Some of the reactions in the educational community were crazy, which, in turn, disconcerted some teachers who wanted to try the method of instruction. Almost at the same time, the Khan Academy, which was then funded by Bill Gates, was becoming all the rage and the anti-reform movement looked for any way possible to undermine this online educational website simply because it was tied to Bill and Melinda Gates. But momentum shifted to the side of the flipped classroom proposal. Although *"old school"* educators wanted to ignore it, the flipped method began to catch on. There were, and still are, critics who feel it is a passing fad, but many teachers and school leaders see the benefits, and consequently, parents and students will reap those benefits.

CONNECTED MOMENT

Have you ever flipped your classroom? Have you watched a video to enhance your understanding of this important concept?

Sending students a lecture or video highlighting a lesson before a class discussion provides teachers with the opportunity to use valuable class time to engage in dialogue or experiments. Students do the prep work for homework ahead of time, giving them a surface-level understanding of the subject matter, which then allows them to come to class ready to ask questions. By virtue of the flipped classroom method, most of the students arrive in a class prepared for more in-depth conversations and learning with the guidance of their teacher. On the flip side of this process, when the students are at home, they have the ability to watch the video or lecture several times facilitating better note-taking and research to raise their level of understanding. Involved parents can also watch the video and get a sense of what their children are learning. We need learning to be at the center of what we do in the classroom and in our schools. Every stakeholder in the school community, especially parents and students, should understand why they are learning what they are learning. Even more, they should have a say in the process. In his book *Visible Learning for Teachers*, John Hattie (2012) talks about the process of making learning visible. Students can ask the following questions:

- Where am I going?
- How am I going?
- Where to next?

In an effective flipped classroom model, learning intentions are clear, students can see where they are going, and the learning process is visible to everyone involved; it makes learning transparent. There is simply no downside to that kind of environment.

 **CONNECTED MOMENT**

Before you begin the flipped process or encourage teachers to engage in it, make certain you have clear learning intentions. At the beginning of this book, I outlined learning intentions. Use them as an example. We should always begin by knowing where we are going, and why we are going.

IS FLIPPING A PASSING FAD?

Many educators thought that the flipped model was a passing fad. It was simply the flavor of the month in new ideas in education. Whenever technology is part of the equation, there will always be educators who provide one thousand reasons why it won't work. Unfortunately for them, and fortunately for our students, this "fad" is not going away. Nor should it, because there are many important reasons to adopt this model. The process helps connect students to resources that in the past required them to go to a library, find a card catalog, search for the book, and hope that the books were not checked out by another student. In the flipped model, students are able to watch a video several times if they need remediation, or once if they are already on track. Using successful flipped classrooms of instruction, technology is properly modeled to students and shows those students that their teachers really do understand their generation.

Through social media, educators share their flipped lessons. It creates this vast community of learners, and subsequently, teachers establish their own PLN's with teachers that they may never meet in person. Any good educator knows that some of their best teaching lessons were the ones they received from others, and the thousands of teachers who are beginning to use the flip model are getting some great ideas from colleagues near and far. As the flipped experience becomes more and popular, they are sharing lessons on Facebook, Pinterest (a pinboard-style photo-sharing website), and Twitter. It has injected exciting life into public and private education and provided a way for students to learn new information, or find remedial ways to learn information at their level. The whole approach inspired me to write the following blog.

A New Approach to Teaching? The Flipped Classroom

> The old image of a teacher is one where they keep their lesson plan books at the end of the school year and do not take the time and effort to change their lessons year after year.

Have you ever woken up and just wanted to do something different? As an educator, do you long to do one thing new in your instructional practice with students? The old image of a teacher suggests a person who recycles her or his lesson plan books from year to year and does not take the time or effort to change those lessons. Or, he or she walk to their filing cabinet and grab the lesson for the day as his or her students sit in rows waiting for instruction. That image is changing rapidly because some teachers are flipping the way they teach long-standing subjects.

As a teacher, I always threw out my lesson plan book after the school year ended because I wanted to do things differently every year. That is very unlike the way I approach my personal life, because I am a creature of habit. As we get older and spend more time in education, that feeling of doing the same thing over and over again happens often, but we have less of an excuse these days not to grow because of the 24–7 connections that we make around us. Twenty minutes a day on Twitter or discussions with your PLN can help you break out of even the toughest of ruts. We need to challenge ourselves to think differently, even if it scares us.

The Windsor Knot

I'm not a fan of wearing ties. As a principal, I know I should like to wrap one of those festive garments around my neck, but I don't. In an effort to mix it up and trick myself into thinking I like ties, I go to YouTube and search for ways to tie different types of knots. Windsor knots always sounded classy, so I figured I would give one of those a shot. In two minutes, I learned how to tie a Windsor knot by watching a video on YouTube.

Don't get me wrong, I still don't like to wear ties, but it helped me stop wearing the same knot day after day after day. It broke me out of my "*Groundhog Day*" mornings and inspired me to step outside of my comfort zone and try something new. I know that makes me sound like a real risk taker, but I try to do one thing per day that breaks me out of a routine.

Many of us get used to our routine, and it makes us feel better when we follow the same pattern on a daily basis. We take the same route to work, eat the same small breakfast, and do the same workout day after day. Unfortunately, that monotony can make us feel very stale, and as educators it can really make for a boring classroom learning environment where our students end up suffering the consequences.

I enjoy watching "How To" videos to learn how to do new things. A YouTube video I watched a couple of years ago was a gateway into watching other informational videos that helped me through my day. If I can't figure something out on my cell phone or iPad, I simply Google search to find a video that helps me solve the problem. If I know it's an

(Continued)

(Continued)

issue I may have again in the future, I save the video so I can review how to solve it when the problem arises again.

Mixing It Up

> I'm a bit wary/skeptical about this whole "Flipped Classroom" idea and how it works in practice. (Ferlazzo, 2012)

The past year has generated a great deal of conversation around the flipped classroom model. As I studied more and more blogs, I became increasingly interested in the concept, but couldn't get past whether it was a new fad or a tried and true approach to educating students. After a great deal of reading, I came to realize that how well it works and the integrity of the model all depend on how educators use the model in their classrooms.

In *Flip Your Classroom: Reach Every Student in Every Class Every Day*, by Aaron Sams and Jonathan Bergmann, the flipped classroom approach is not just about students watching their teacher on video. (Think of me and my Windsor knot video as only half the method!) The students watch the lecture in the comfort of their home and then delve deeper into the lecture the following day through a lab, a follow-up activity, or some other classroom conversation (Bergmann & Sams, 2012).

In typical teaching practices, students listen to a lecture at school and then are assigned the follow-up activity alone at home where a teacher cannot help them if they have difficulties. The flipped approach changes it around so that students watch the lecture alone and then go to class where the teacher is there to help.

If educators videotape themselves lecturing and then offer it to students, there are a variety of things that can happen. Many students may review it over and over again at their pace and really learn something valuable. In addition, students may be more engaged because they understand their teachers are incorporating the use of technology to help them learn.

However, if the taped lesson isn't very engaging, students may find it painful to watch. If someone is going to do a flipped lesson, they should make sure they have fun with it. A bad lecture in person is bad enough. Having one taped that a student has to watch over and over again should not be a waste of time. Educators shouldn't do it just to say they did it. They should try the flipped approach because they really want to find a way to engage their students.

Battling the Cynic

The cynic in me wants to say that the Flipped Classroom model is really nothing new. I consider myself a connected educator and have long tried to use technology in both my instruction as a teacher as well as a principal. There are many of us that no longer look at technology as a tool to use, but as a natural part of our day. It's like an extension of our arm . . . and many times our brain.

The flipped model is supposed to allow teachers the opportunity to provide a more individualized learning system for their students. Students can watch the lesson at home and in class, ask questions, and have better conversations. It is important to remember that whatever teachers decide, the first time they try the process it will not be perfect and they need to keep experimenting to see how they can evolve and perfect the use of the model.

All in all, it is about offering a student-centered approach to learning. However, one of the other benefits is that it may also provide the opportunity for teachers to break out of the rut of teaching the same lessons day after day and year after year. It forces them to step outside their comfort zone, and then all students benefit from that expansion.

....

Source: http://blogs.edweek.org/edweek/finding_common_ground/2012/08/a_new_approach_to_teaching_the_flipped_classroom.html?qs=flipped+classroom

FLIPPING OUT THE CLASSROOM

As a school leader, I wanted my teachers to use the flipped model. After writing the blog in the summer of 2012, I approached our fifth grade teachers about flipping. One teacher seemed interested. We talked about how it wasn't a passing fad, and that it might be interesting to try it a few times. After all, we had several technological tools at our fingertips and our school district used edline, a K–12 web-based communication solution that is a password protected parent portal where teachers post assignments on their edline page and have direct access to the e-mail addresses of the parents who signed up for edline.

After some group discussions at grade-level meetings and faculty meetings, a few other teachers began to flip their instruction. As the months went on, teachers found new ways to incorporate flipping their classroom when it made sense. Whether it was a short historical video they posted to Edline for their students to watch, a blog they posted and students had to respond to the comment section, or a science passage that went home first before they participated in a lab the next day, the flipped method began to thrive. I wanted teachers to adopt the method naturally, and not simply because I requested it. From everything I read in blogs and articles and watched in videos, I really loved the idea of teachers using this method to engage students and make learning more visible, and our teachers were putting those ideas into action. One of the benefits was that parents could see what their children were learning, and it helped prepare them for parent-teacher conferences (our teachers flipped those as well!).

Teachers began to focus more on student-led conferences, as opposed to the typical parent-teacher conference. It was something they had been doing before I became the school leader, but they stepped away from it when the new rules of accountability began to be enforced in schools. They wanted to play it safe for a year or two because everything seemed so unstable. Fortunately, the flipped method, and the strength to step outside their comfort zone, helped them reestablish that focus.

Preparing for student-led conferences really starts at the beginning of the school year. As the quarter or trimester goes on, students collect their favorite pieces of work and add them to a portfolio. More technologically advanced schools may incorporate online portfolios instead of hard copies in folders.

Great writing assignments, art projects, or anything that focuses on the strength of a child can be added to a portfolio for use during a student-led conference. Depending on the age, children need to know what comprises a good portfolio addition because they often want to add everything they do, which would be overwhelming.

As the conference time approaches, the teacher spends time with the class discussing the best pieces to include in their portfolios. Students decorate their portfolio and add a table of contents so that everyone who views the portfolio knows its contents.

During the conference time, the teacher usually sets up a 30 to 40 minute conference with the parents. The first 15 to 20 minutes of the conference is between the child and her or his parent. Parents sit in a designated spot with their child, and they are lead through the portfolio. This is an important time for parents to have questions for their children and to fully engage in the process. When parents can't attend or do not show up for the conference, perhaps another teacher (librarian, reading teacher, music teacher, etc.) or the principal can meet with the child during a non-conference day to go through the portfolio.

After the parent and child work through the portfolio, the teacher meets with the child and parent. The teacher may discuss the portfolio and talk with the parent about the work that was good as well as areas where the child can improve. The purpose of the conference is to provide children with a full picture of how they are doing in class. It helps to build maturity with the student as well as give them an opportunity to discuss their own learning.

(Continued)

(Continued)

In order to properly engage students in their own learning we must allow them the opportunity to be a part of the conference between a teacher and parent. Allowing them to choose their own pieces for a portfolio adds to the concept that the child is the center of the learning process.

As students get older they are at risk to become less engaged in school, and student-led conferences allow them to be fully engaged in the process. It also helps parents communicate better with their children, and perhaps can even help parents feel more engaged in their child's academic progress as well (Pierce-Picciotto, 1996).

In some schools, student-led conferences may be something that teachers cannot initiate presently because of time constraints, but they should consider adopting this format in the future. Perhaps teachers can make it a goal for a spring conference, or the next school year. The time devoted to student-led conferences is time well spent.

....

Source: http://blogs.edweek.org/edweek/finding_common_ground/2011/11/student-led_conferences.html

IN THE END

Flipped leadership requires school leaders to encourage teachers to step outside their comfort zone and to inspire them to try new ways to engage students. Involving students in the process is just one way of meeting that need. In our present system of accountability and unfunded mandates, it's not easy to introduce innovative practices because teachers want to play it safe. Unfortunately, playing it safe doesn't always allow us to maximize our student engagement, and after a while, our practices become old and stale. We should embrace technology and help our school community see the benefits of being connected.

The greatest part about the flipped classroom is that teachers can actualize the process anyway that they desire. Too often, in our effort to not fail, we all want to make sure we are doing things the right way or have a fear of getting the wrong answer. In the flipped model, there is no right answer. Whatever is done to maximize learning in the classroom is acceptable and beneficial. Teachers can post a blog, send a video, or post a link that brings students to a new research article; and students can view those methods once or numerous times, and then go to class the next day with a deeper level of understanding so that with their teacher as the guide, they can dive even deeper into learning. There is no one way to flip, and as much as I encouraged it with some staff members, I realized that there was one person who was not practicing what they preached—me—so I had to change my habits.

ACTION STEPS

- Send out some articles as resources to highlight the flipped classrooms. Do a Google search and post the blogs I used as vignettes, or find a few written by Jonathan Bergmann and Aaron Sams.
- Use a faculty meeting to discuss the flipped method of instruction. Allow teachers time to share best practices.
  - ○ Talk about barriers
  - ○ Pros and cons
  - ○ Provide resources
- Focus on one area of technology at each faculty meeting. Many teachers don't know where to start.
- Have an expectation that technology will be used. I would venture to guess that most teachers have smartphones, which means they value technology at least in one part of their lives.

The Flipped
Faculty Meeting

As a few of the teachers began using the flipped method to engage students, I received my very own challenge. The following vignette tells that story.

How to Flip a Faculty Meeting

Faculty meetings are as good or as bad as we want them to be. Some faculty meetings can be a time when there are great discussions about education and we feel as though we are a part in the movie *Dead Poet's Society*. Other times, they are an example of bad behavior because adults have sidebars or they argue back and forth, or worse

(Continued)

they remind us of the famous scene in the movie *Ferris Bueller's Day Off* where Ben Stein plays the economics teacher who just drones on and on.

My faculty meetings are awesome. I send out an agenda 24 hours before the meeting so the staff can see the list of items to review. At the beginning of the year, teachers and administrators sign up for specific months to bring food. There are some awesome cooks and bakers in my school, so the food is always top-notch for the meetings. We used to have the faculty meetings in the morning before the students arrived, but last year we switched to the afternoons.

I love my staff, and getting together doesn't happen as often as it should. The faculty meetings last about 45 minutes; sometimes depending on the list of items, we can finish in 30 minutes. Over the years, I have included quick videos to make people laugh during more stressful months. Other times, the meetings are quiet because people are overwhelmed, so we get those meetings over as quickly as possible.

Unfortunately, I came to the conclusion this summer that my meetings, although nice, are not always worth the time the faculty takes to attend them, so I decided to flip them this year. Don't get me wrong, the faculty meetings are not that bad, but I want them to be different. During a year with so many changes in education, I need them to be different.

Why Flip the Faculty Meeting?

I have read a great deal about flipping the classroom (Bergmann & Sams, 2012), and I was concerned it was more of a fad than anything worthwhile. However, the more the cynic in me stayed out of the way, the more the creative side thought that this was a good model to use. Flipping the classroom can take the lecture out of the classroom and replace it with more in-depth conversations about important topics.

Teachers are using the flipped approach, so like any good principal, I sent my fifth grade teachers the challenge of trying the model during this school year. Then, the plan somehow backfired on me because David Culberhouse, a senior director of elementary education in California (The Next Step), sent me a challenge through Twitter. He asked me when I was going to flip my faculty meetings, and he referenced a blog he read the month before.

After reading North Carolina teacher Bill Ferriter's *Tempered Radical Blog,* he posed a challenge to principals to flip their meetings, so this year I'm accepting the challenge. A few weeks ago, I researched different software to use to engage the staff. I have presided over a few webinars and enjoy using links, videos, and PowerPoint presentations, hence I decided to initiate my project by using TouchCast, which is an integrated platform for the creation and playback of interactive videos.

In about fifteen minutes, I created a TouchCast video of all the items I thought staff should know at our first faculty meeting (i.e., procedures, dates and notes from the office, etc.). In the recording, I told staff that we would meet on the first day of school in our first official faculty meeting to discuss the Annual Professional Performance Review Plan (APPR), the Common Core State Standards (CCSS), and the New York State Growth Model for Educator Evaluation.

Those topics are very important to our existence as educators right now, and the faculty meeting is the most important place to discuss those issues. Every principal and staff has topics they should discuss at length, so the flipped model is worth trying once to see if it makes those faculty conversations more authentic.

Step Outside Your Comfort Zone

It seems in education that there are many reasons not to step outside our comfort zones and try something new. It's an easy time to play it

(Continued)

(Continued)

safe and keep faculty meetings short and to the point. Unfortunately we are teaching our staff that risk taking isn't worth it anymore, and that is the wrong message to send. There is one major reason not to follow the status quo . . . *our school community.*

Our students deserve more than people who play it safe, and our staffs deserve principals who lead the way by trying something innovative. Principals set the tone every day in their schools and communities and the flipped model can represent a symbolic way of telling adults that we still have to be innovative. It is really hard for a principal to preach innovation if they aren't using it in the venues they lead. Try it once and see what happens.

Source: http://blogs.edweek.org/edweek/finding_common_ground/2012/09/the_flipped_faculty_meeting.html

I realized after Bill Ferriter's blog that I expected something out of my staff that I did not expect out of myself. Unfortunately, I also realized that I was intimidated to try something new with my staff, even though they were extremely supportive of my leadership. It wasn't the actual flipping process that caused my issue, but the expectation that staff would watch it and be able to engage further in a faculty meeting setting. Fortunately, since my tenure began in 2006, I continually sent out research-based articles along with blogs in order to spark a conversation, but it wasn't considered flipping because I didn't really have any expectation that the staff would read the information. I know that sounds absurd, but teachers are busy; therefore I wanted to provide the information, but leave it up to them whether they used it or not. However, the conversations in the hallway and in the faculty room told me that they were definitely reading them.

Some of the articles were controversial, while others merely suggested some new research. I tried selecting articles, blogs, and videos that covered a wide range of topics and met the needs of diverse mindsets. When it came to the flipped faculty meetings, I sent out teacher instructional videos that we were going to watch together and critique. I sent out YouTube presentations by leadership expert and author Todd Whitaker; talks that we could discuss in person; or an important Ted talk by education expert Sir Ken Robinson called *How Schools Kill Creativity* (2006). I wanted my faculty and staff to watch it, and then we could discuss how to construct more creative learning experiences for our students.

Using the flipped leadership method led us to deeper discussions where new ideas were introduced to take a break from the real—and perceived—accountability we face every day. It helped us build a more positive morale that focused on creativity, fun, and learning, instead of the idea that we could no longer have fun in our elementary school. Flipped leadership helped inspire collective thoughts to change stakeholders from being victims in the educational process, to change agents of learning.

In addition, I looked to teachers for resources. If a teacher provided me with a link, I would send that out so we could discuss it. This wasn't all willy-nilly. There was a process and intention behind the flipped videos, but I didn't refer to it as flipped faculty meetings because we didn't always discuss the links I sent out, and that is the key ingredient in the flipped process. Leaders must have a learning intention and expectations behind the video or article they flip, and then it must be discussed at the faculty meeting. Faculty need to leave the meeting with *take-aways*.

When I started my first formal flipped process, I remember thinking that if I was nervous to try it with my staff, I could only imagine that other school leaders would be intimidated as well. I sent the first flipped video before our initial faculty meeting of the 2012–2013 school year. I added the names of new staff, some important dates, and the typical beginning of the year rules. I even added in some pictures to illustrate what had been happening at the school over the summer. It was meant to create a fresh and innovative start to the school year. A new tone was set for teachers, and hopefully for students. What was the result? To put it mildly, it tanked. I knew by the views that only about 10 of the 50 staff watched it, and that could also mean that 5 staff members watched it twice. I was disappointed, and a bit embarrassed.

One of the errors I made was that I created the first flipped video while teachers were not contractually obligated to be at school, which meant that they received an unfamiliar link. As much as I explained the process in the e-mail I sent out, some of the teachers were away the week before school started so they didn't open the video until the day we had our first meeting, if they opened it at all. That is probably the moment that most leaders would retreat, declare defeat, and never create a flipped faculty meeting again. I was bound and determined to make a flipped faculty meeting successful.

● ● ● ● REFLECTION

When flipping your faculty meeting, make certain you prepare your staff by letting them know exactly what you are doing, why you're doing it, and that you have the expectation that they will watch it so that they are prepared for the faculty meeting. Perhaps you can send out a link to a blog or article about the process so they can go a bit deeper with their understanding. It also helps if you make the video as engaging as possible.

As time went on, I began using TouchCast in the flipped faculty meeting process so I could send out important updates in a formal way so that faculty had all the information they needed for the next faculty meeting. The ideas came out of our PAC meetings. We started PAC in 2006 when I started my tenure as the principal, and I was not always in agreement with the two co-chairs. At PAC, we had a respectful level of discourse from time to time depending on what was happening in education or in our district.

In 2012, I decided that I would ask PAC to come up with topics they wanted to learn more about at the faculty meetings. Considering PAC involved stakeholders from the whole school community, I knew they would talk with their grade-level peers to get ideas. I began to take those ideas and use them in our flipped faculty meetings. For full disclosure, I did not flip the meeting every month. I didn't want to make it a novelty and knew I needed to get more staff on board. There is not one single way to flip a faculty meeting, so I mixed it up as much as possible. Perhaps it was videos one month or articles the next. We agreed on the focus in PAC, and I found resources to meet our needs. It didn't double our workload, but made our time together more precious.

● ● ● ● REFLECTION

What would you choose to flip? What topics are most important? Think of topics that need more time, and the benefit of true dialogue with staff. That is the topic you should flip.

ONE FLIP LEADS TO ANOTHER

John Hattie (2012) often talks about the idea that teachers should be creating dialogue and not monologue in their classroom instruction. Too often, instruction involves a monologue, where the teacher stands at the front of the room or walks around and the students are guests in their own learning. Dialogue means that all participants are actively engaged and there is a back and forth happening. Faculty meetings should be the same. Considering Hattie views "*dialogue and not monologue*" as a "Mind Frame," which is at the infrastructure of making learning visible, I realized that I needed to do the same for faculty meetings. What I found is that when we were more engaged in our meetings, it was the flipped model that led to those intense discussions.

Certainly, not everyone participated, but most of the staff did. I also knew by the views on the TouchCast that I uploaded to my YouTube page that many staff members were watching. The faculty meetings we had were some of the best in my leadership career. I never walk into the room thinking I'm the smartest guy there, and I definitely don't walk into a shared decision-making session (SDM) and expect everyone to abide with my idea. Shared decision making in many buildings means that the school leader is interested only if you share in his or her idea. Flipping the faculty meetings gave us the opportunity to really discuss issues and walk away with ideas.

You may think that your flipped leadership experience ends within the walls of your school, but it shouldn't. During that first trial year, it never occurred to me that there was a stakeholder population that was in my blind spot. Making connections with students was easy, because I walked into the classrooms every single day and was out at recess, bus duty, and lunch. Making connections with parents was much harder, and while I was in the process of flipping faculty meetings, I never thought that I should take the time to flip my communication with parents. But then the sky started to fall, and I realized I had to flip my communication outside of our school walls.

ACTION STEPS

- Use your building-level team to develop a focus for each and every faculty meeting.
- List the topics that the faculty wants to discuss. Some of the following are examples:
  - Sharing best practices in the Common Core
  - Evidence-based observations
  - Classroom observation process
  - How to focus on making learning visible
  - How to best communicate with parents
  - Classroom management
  - Student engagement

- Create a monthly calendar at the beginning of the year that has the faculty focus. It provides you time to find quality resources and gives your faculty time to see what topics are coming.
- Use *Today's Meet* (a backchannel, which helps teachers conduct online discussions, while channeling the results onto one web page or an interactive whiteboard) in the faculty meeting. It's a free service. Simply name your meeting, keep it open for a few hours, days, weeks or a year, and faculty members

can provide feedback to the meeting, either during the meeting or after they have time to reflect.

● Set the expectation that staff participate in one way or another. After all, we are lifelong learners and need to participate in our own learning.

When enacting the flipped faculty model, consider the following:

● **Why are you flipping your meeting?** Don't do it because it is the new thing to do. Flip your meeting because you want to focus on a couple of topics more at length in the actual meeting.

● **How long do you record yourself?** It seems like 15 minutes isn't a long time, but it is when you're the one watching someone else talk. Don't do it for that long. Try to keep the flipped portion down to 5 minutes or less. Remember, the flipped portion is setting the stage for the actual meeting. It's not meant to make meetings longer, but more productive.

● **What are you using to flip your meeting?** Principals have to use technology that they are familiar and comfortable with—I ended up using TouchCast because it was extremely user-friendly. TouchCast allowed me to record myself using pictures and 30-second video clips at the same time that I recorded my voice. There are many other comparable tools out there.

● **Who benefits from the experience?** Both the principal and the staff should benefit from the experience. I'm not an expert because I have only done it once, but I am planning on tackling different topics in different ways through the flipped model.

● **What topics need more discussion?** It's easy right now to find topics that need more discussion. APPR and CCSS are two topics I felt needed our time and effort. During a year, there are many topics worth discussing at length.

CHAPTER
4

Flipping Parent Communication

● ● ● ● REFLECTION

Take the time to reflect on all the ways you communicate with parents. Think of your monthly newsletters and the events you want the parents in your school community to know about. How can you be proactive and provide them with information ahead of time so that they can ask you questions when you see them? Ask yourself whether you want them to ask you questions . . . or do you just want them to have the information?

In July 2012, all schools in New York State were required to have anti-bullying policies in place. It was called the Dignity for All Students Act (DASA), and it stipulated that all public schools in

New York State were required to have board policies and school codes of conduct that included language regarding sexual orientation and gender expression, among many other areas. For many schools across the state, this was a very big initiative because it was the first time they were required to address the issues of a marginalized population like sexual orientation. Additionally, schools were required to communicate this new law to parents at an open meeting.

In addition to DASA, schools were negotiating their way through the adoption of the Common Core State Standards (CCSS). Together, they were two profound initiatives, and I wanted to make certain that parents knew about them before they attended our yearly Open House, so I flipped the information about the two initiatives using TouchCast, and sent it out to them through our Edline parent portal.

Many school leaders in our state did not want to address the initiatives that way. It was easier to send home a flyer, or perhaps prepare nothing at all. After all, the DASA and Common Core police did not exist, and school leaders sometimes like to take the path of least resistance, especially at the beginning of the school year. Fortunately, I worked in a school district that wanted to communicate these two initiatives, and I felt like flipping communication was the best way to approach it. In all honesty however, I did not think it was going to work.

I downloaded a few pictures from Google, and then used a Word document to get my thoughts together. The great aspect of using TouchCast is that they have a "Green Screen" option which allows the user to put a picture up so their face doesn't have to appear on camera. I did not want the message to be about me. I wanted the message to be about . . . the message. Since putting the idea of flipping communication out on blogs and through Twitter, I have seen examples where principals talk "on the fly." I cannot do that because I like to prepare what I say on a video. In this particular situation, and where it concerned Open House, I recorded several versions before sending it out. I was actually fairly nervous to try this new method of communication with parents. What if it failed? What if no one watched it? What if I got a flood of e-mails saying they disagreed with DASA or wanted to meet with me right away? After all, e-mails are instantaneous, and we can never really predict how parents will react.

Truth be told, most school leaders and teachers believe that parents do not read newsletters. It's one of those forms of communication that school personnel have been using for decades, but it's typically one-sided. Leaders and teachers believe that many parents are so distracted by their own careers and nightly sporting events that they are disengaged from the school community, but they send out newsletters any way because it "proves" they're communicating with families. I think quite the opposite, and firmly believe that we need to not only send out newsletters that are engaging, we also have to find other innovative ways to communicate with parents in our community. However, although I hoped for the best, I wasn't completely confident that my 5-minute video would work.

● ● ● ● REFLECTION

Think of an initiative idea that you want parents in your school community to know about. Perhaps it involves a focus on learning, or an upcoming school event, such as an Open House or parent-teacher conference. Write up a short Word document about what you want to say. Find some fun pictures that can be on the screen as you record your voice. Make it fun and informative. If you don't like it . . . try it again. Send it out. Just remember that it won't be perfect the first time. It's not meant to be as entertaining as a Super Bowl commercial.

Within minutes I received positive responses through e-mail. Parents loved the video and valued the information I sent, and I always respond when a parent e-mails me, even if it is to say thank you. Although they still had questions, they said they would wait until Open House. When the night of Open House came, parents showed up to the event with prior information thanks to the flipped video, and they came with their questions. A few people came over to me before we officially began and asked me to send out more flipped videos. I remember feeling like the idea worked and that I was on to something special.

It's typically standing room only at our Poestenkill, New York, events, but this was better than that. The parents who attended were more present than in the past. They were not passively sitting in their seats looking to get through my monologue in order to get to see their child's teacher, which was why they really showed up. The parents actually had questions specific to the CCSS and DASA. We had dialogue about bullying and discussed what constitutes bullying and what does not. It was helpful that I had previously written *Dignity for All: Safeguarding LGBT Students* (DeWitt, 2012a) and had covered the subjects in some blogs for *Education Week* that I know the parents had read, but that wasn't the only reason we seemed to have open communication. It was as if they knew I went a little deeper in my communication, and they wanted to go a little deeper in their participation in Open House. We actually had parents stay behind to ask some more questions or provide feedback on the video I sent out. I knew then that flipping communication was a successful way to get out information to the school community.

It was the best Open House experience of my leadership career. I left the meeting feeling inspired, and a bit relieved, and looking forward to the next issue I could address through flipped communication. The greatest thing about using Edline to send out the video was that I had the flexibility to include other administrators in the district and our staff so that everyone could read what I was distributing. The process was very successful, and I knew I could effectively use it again. At that moment though, I did not realize how much of a personal impact this communication venue could have on people—how well it could meet my needs as well as the needs of the parents. It became more than just a way to talk about initiatives and mandates; it became a way to give parents a window into the world of learning.

MAKING LEARNING VISIBLE

Soon after the Open House, I began to send home other notifications to keep parents informed about hot topics. Whether it was more about DASA or clarifying information about CCSS, I wanted to go deeper with my own leadership and connect with parents in a variety of ways. It wasn't that I believed 100 percent of the parents were viewing the videos, but I did know that there was a solid percentage of parents who were watching them. To me, flipping parent communication came with the same expectations I had for the newsletters that were sent out. I could provide the information, but it was up to the parents to take the time to read them or watch the videos. My job was to make them engaging.

And then something else happened which made me realize that flipping communication had additional benefits. A parent contacted me about the lack of communication she felt she had with her child's teacher. As the school leader with an open door policy, sometimes parents come to me to ask advice on how to best approach a subject with their child's teacher. Keep in mind that many parents believe that if they address a problem with a teacher, their child may suffer the consequences. Although that may not be true in most cases, it still can happen, which is why many parents first go to the principal.

In this case, most of the communication between the teacher and parent was either misunderstood or twisted around. In an effort to remedy the situation, I asked her to meet with the teacher and myself. Technology is such a great tool, but when the communication is going in a negative direction there is nothing better than a face-to-face meeting, or at least a phone call. Sending an e-mail sometimes makes it too easy to try to "one-up" the other person or say things we would never say in person. It's also very easy when people are angry to read tone into an e-mail that was not intended. It is always a good idea to walk away from a bad e-mail and give yourself time to reflect on how to answer it.

I felt that if the parent, the teacher, and I met in person, we could work it all out. The meeting started out peacefully, but it soon turned defensive. It was like a fast moving train that I couldn't stop. When I indicated that the meeting was over because we clearly were not going to come to an understanding, the parent began crying. She said she wasn't *"like the parents who could volunteer during the school day,"* and she just wanted to know how her child was doing every day. According to Stephen Covey (1989), one of the seven habits of highly effective people is to *"Seek first to understand, then to be understood."* I realized that in an effort to explain our side, I hadn't been listening to the side of the parent.

I remember feeling completely focused on her words, and I said, *"I hear you saying that you can't get to school and you're frustrated because you want to be here, but can't."* She continued crying, and the kindergarten teacher leaned over and gave the parent her cell phone number. She told the parent to text her throughout the day if she had questions. The cell phone number came with conditions, but the parent stopped crying and then began to smile. She had a mother's guilt, and we had a breakthrough. I refer to those as *"Dr. Phil Moments,"* even though I am not a regular Dr. Phil viewer. Fortunately, the meeting ended better than it began.

However, that meeting helped me determine to send out to parents more than just updates to new school initiatives. It was then that I decided to make learning visible to our parents in the school community. Over the next few months, I went around school and took pictures of students engaged in learning and then returned to my office to create a TouchCast called *"The Day in the Life of a Poestenkill Student."* Traditionally, we had parent release forms in place giving permission to have their children in pictures that may end up on the district website. I do a lot of work with WNYT, our Albany NBC affiliate, and they often came out to the school to shoot a "B-roll" after an interview. A B-roll is the term used for footage that news stations play while the newscaster isn't on air and their voice is dubbed into a shot. I did not take pictures of the students without parental permission.

It's amazing how much goes on in school during the day, and although I'm the principal, I soon realized how much material was worthy of a TouchCast video to send home to parents. Schools have so many busy working parents who cannot make it to school during the day, and flipping communication gave them a window into the world of learning that their children were experiencing, and it gave them some conversation pieces to bring up at the dinner table when they were home with their children. They were able to take the dialogue far past *"What did you do today?"* and focus on asking specific questions about what they knew their children learned that day. I did my best to include all grade levels and subjects. It was a way to bring our community closer, especially after a few years of devastating budget cuts, teacher and administrator lay-offs, and increased accountability and mandates. This proved to be a wonderful way to circle the wagons in our district and become an integral part of the community.

CONNECTED MOMENT

I use TouchCast to flip my communication. If you're going to flip your leadership, find some vehicle that you are comfortable with because that comfort level makes a big difference in your approach. Find your own style.

BUILD A BETTER HOME-SCHOOL PARTNERSHIP

As school leaders, everything we do is interrelated. We lack the luxury to ignore our parents through the hard times and must work out whatever issues come our way. If we don't try to make our school community stronger and more open, then we should not be in the position of school leader. Over the past few years, many educators and schools have experienced hard times. Whether its budget cuts, unfunded mandates, or increased accountability, our school climates have taken a negative hit. The rhetoric about the public school system often turns to how we are failing and not preparing our students for the 21st century, even though we are already a decade and a half into the century. In my own district, we have seen tremendously hard times.

A few years ago, as we recognized that our enrollment was going down and our budget cuts were increasing, our superintendent and the board of education agreed to close a one classroom per grade-level school that had been annexed into our district fifteen years before. It was a decision made over a few months and it was not a decision that was welcomed by that school's community. Although the school district began the process of creating a stakeholder group to discuss the school closure, no one thought it would happen within a few months. Parents and children picketed the board meetings, the news stations attended every one of those sessions, a hate blog about school administrators was created, and when our administrative team held an open forum for questions and answers, the meetings quickly deteriorated into negativism and abuse. Adults were screaming at us, calling us names, and saying we didn't care about their children.

The bad press continued because we were ahead of the curve of other school districts that were going to be forced to close a school. It was not a healthy and fun place to be, and I still shudder when I think about some of those moments. Unfortunately, the entire school community from the closed school was going to relocate to Poestenkill School—all of the students, and the few very angry parents. Although we had numerous events to try to bring us all together, for the first year after the transition it was very hard and there were a lot of negative feelings. Over time, the hurt began to disappear, although both parents and students will probably always miss their first school. As a school leader, we inevitably face experiences of that nature from time to time, but I can assure you that it is not something we learn in our leadership training.

Flipping my communication with parents was another way to try to reach and get passed the school closing that took place a few years before. The events were indirectly related because students, teachers, and parents left one school where they had annual events and a special bond and had to come to a school where they felt as though they had to give up their school identity and blend in with ours at Poestenkill. It was always my goal to try to figure out how to begin new annual events together. Flipping communication was something I had never done before the school closing, and it became a way to highlight why our school was stronger with both communities together.

In *Digital Leadership: Changing Paradigms for Changing Times*, Eric Sheninger wrote that leaders should "*Share as many student and teacher accomplishments and success stories as possible. Parents want and need to hear the great things happening in our buildings and classrooms*" (2014, p. 87). That advice became even truer after our consolidation. I needed parents to see that their children were engaged and happy and that the transition opened their children up to meeting new friends. Whether a school goes through a merger or not, parents need to be engaged in the process of learning. Images convey meaning, and the images sent out through flipped communication can help parents feel a sense of safety, a sense of pride, and a sense of involvement, even when they can't get to school on a regular basis.

The following vignette illustrates the art of flipping parent communication.

Take a Risk . . . Flip Your Parent Communication!

The Flipped model can clearly be a fad, but it doesn't have to be if it is done with integrity.

Old model of parent communication. Monthly newsletters with important dates & information

New model of parent communication. Classroom websites, district Facebook pages, school Twitter pages . . . and monthly newsletters.

(Continued)

(Continued)

But What About Flipping Communication?

Most schools are looking for new and innovative ways to engage parents. Connected leaders flip their faculty meetings in order to model

the method for teachers who want to flip their classrooms. Some leaders initiate the process because teachers who flip their classrooms have influenced them and inspired them to take a risk. Yes, risk taking is reciprocal.

Unfortunately, due to outside influences, like increased accountability, or inside influences, such as . . . well,

(iStock Photo)

staff and school leaders that don't get along, some school leaders are nervous about flipping anything.

They have a fear that the reaction to flipping will look something like this . . .

Last year I posted a blog about flipping parent communication, and there were mixed reactions. I get it! There are educators who hate discussing technology because they believe it is a fad or feel that techies inflate the need for technology in the classroom. I have written numerous times about finding a balance, so even though I feel that it's implied when I write, I will say it again—it's about finding a balance (finding common ground) between being old school and being . . . *well* . . . new school.

For many educators, when they learned about my flipping faculty meetings or parent communication it sounded to them like an odd thing to do. Accordingly, I received the following questions.

- Was I just trying to put a twist on an old form of communication?
- Was it really necessary to flip communication with parents?
- How many parents actually viewed the videos?

The answer to questions 1 and 2 are both "yes." The answer to question three is a bit more complicated. To my surprise, many parents responded positively. I noticed that the videos I flipped were viewed a lot in the first 24 hours. We can't say the same thing for our paper communication (although we always need to send that because some parents don't have computers). We don't know if the paper we send home gets thrown away without being looked at or hung up on the refrigerator. (We actually call our newsletter The Refrigerator Page.)

When it came to flipping communication, parents contacted me to say they liked the way that I flipped some big events, important information (DASA, Common Core State Standards, etc.), and just a regular day in the life of our students (i.e., showing students in music class, using netbooks, in gym, etc.). To be perfectly honest, I now feel as though I did not flip communication enough.

Why Flip Our Communication?

Parents are really busy and some of them just can't get to school. They miss out on volunteering or have to work when we have night events. Flipping communication allows them to see what they missed. It helps them feel a little more engaged even if they have to work.

If it is a flipped communication about something that happened in the school day, and the school leader sends it out that day, it is quite possible that parents can view it before their child even gets home from school. This, of course, can lead to a dinner conversation. When parents ask, "What did you do at school today?" their child may have a better answer than . . ."Nothin."

A recent Huffington Post Tech blog stated, "*The U.N. telecom agency says there were about 6 billion subscriptions by the end of*

(Continued)

(Continued)

2011—roughly one for 86 of every 100 people." It went on to say, *"2.3 billion people—or about one in three of the world's 7 billion inhabitants—were Internet users by the end of 2011."*

That has staggering implications for schools. Most of our parents, and many of our students, carry a smartphone with them wherever they go. It's important for them to disconnect, but it's just as important for schools to get with society and upgrade their communication systems.

Flipping communication can clearly be a fad, but it doesn't have to be if it is done with integrity. Unfortunately, too many school leaders will not take the chance because they are worried about taking a risk or looking foolish to parents. I guess I wasn't worried about it as much because there are times when I do look foolish and I'm all right with that. However, I also trust our parents because we have a really special community and I figured if the experience was a flop, they would let me know that they didn't like it.

Images Evoke Feeling

Over the past year I have taken a great deal of time to figure out why flipping is important. I don't have any long-term longitudinal studies that state the importance of flipping. There is just too much data in my life these days, and I do not need any more. However, I looked at the process of flipping communication from two different viewpoints:

Viewpoint #1. As I incorporated pictures or videos into the flipped communication, I had parents and teachers stop to tell me what they thought about them. Perhaps the video inspired them in some way or they thought the information was important. The flipped video was something they could watch on their own, and it inspired a conversation.

Viewpoint #2. I attended an edtech conference in Boston, and the keynote presenter chose to use a medium to present that was short on narrative and heavy on pictures. I was completely engrossed in what she was saying because the pictures caught my attention. Pictures have a way of doing that, especially when they are of our students. They get us to smile, and we feel more engaged.

Of course, schools can continue to use a newsletter and do nothing else. However, if that is all they use, they can't walk away wondering why parents aren't as engaged as they want. School leaders, much like the staff they lead, need to take risks. Sure, they might fail once or twice, but if the flipping is done with integrity, it may lead to a new format to engage parents, and we all benefit from that.

Source: http://blogs.edweek.org/edweek/finding_common_ground/2013/07/take_a_risk_flip_your_parent_communication.html

Flipping parent communication opened up a whole new world for our parents, but also for me as a school leader. After putting the idea out on Twitter, I began to write about it more for *Education Week,* and it seemed to strike a chord with parents and school leaders. Comments ranged from *"I've never seen a school leader communicate so much with parents,"* to *"I wish my son's principal would do that."* I simply put a twist on the flipped classroom approach.

During the summer of 2013, I presented for the second time at the National Association for Elementary School Principal's (NAESP) Conference in Baltimore. I presented a workshop on the topic of flipped communication. Soon after the presentation, I began hearing from principals who attended the session, and they too were flipping their parent communication and faculty meetings. On Twitter, I began to see principals take the idea I presented and make it better. Some of the principals had their faces on camera as they talked, while others used the green screen. An even better improvement was when principals began using their students in the process, and then Tweeting out the final product.

The great aspect of Twitter is that it involves open communication, so I saw how parents were responding to leaders who were sending out the flipped communication. It just all made sense, and the parents felt like they were a bigger part of their school community than ever before. Never to rest on my laurels, I began looking for other ways to engage parents, and one of the easiest was an idea I picked up on from Facebook.

FLIPPING PARENT CONFERENCES

Early in the fall of 2013, before I began my leave of absence to work with John Hattie and Corwin's Visible Learning team, I was cruising through Facebook one morning before I left for work, and noticed that one of my former high school classmates mentioned that she hated not getting her child's report card before the parent-teacher conference. She wanted the information ahead of time so that she could digest it and go to the meeting with questions. As I turned off my computer and headed to work, I realized we did the very same thing at my school. All of our elementary schools hold the report card hostage to get parents in for the conference. I contacted my elementary principal colleagues, suggested we send them out two days ahead of time (it was late in the process) and allow parents time to digest the report cards so they could come in better prepared to discuss them.

It worked. We didn't have parents suddenly cancel because they had what they needed. We actually had parents who came prepared because we encouraged them to do so. We treated them like adults and let go of our control issues. We flipped the way we did parent-teacher conferences and it worked. Below is a vignette highlighting the idea of flipped parent conferences.

---------- Flipping Parent Conferences?

I venture to guess that if we treat parents like they are going to do the right thing instead of assuming they will do the wrong thing, many parents will rise to the challenge.

Many educators are fairly tired of hearing about flipped classrooms, flipped parent communication, and flipped faculty meetings. I'm sure they would prefer to take out the word *flipped* and replace it with another word. As much as the flipped method is loved by some and hated by others, it really makes a great deal of sense.

Providing students with links and resources before a classroom discussion, or to further a classroom discussion, is such a great way to deepen learning in the classroom. Flipping faculty meetings provides the same benefit to teachers and staff. And quite frankly, flipping parent communication has been one of the most unique and worthwhile ways I have communicated with parents in my district.

But . . . Flipping Parent Conferences?

So . . . we decided to flip our parent conferences. It's not what you think. There are no engaging videos or educational articles to watch and study before the conference. Flipping conferences is more about providing parents with what they need to be prepared for the conference.

We decided to send home all report cards before the parent-teacher conferences, and not after. I realize that many schools may already do this, but many schools do not. Holding report cards until parent-teacher conferences used to be a way to get parents to attend their conference and not cancel. Basically, teachers (under the guise of their school leader) held report cards hostage in order to get parents to attend.

My hope was that sending report cards home with a letter about them would inspire parents to review the report cards and come in with questions, making the parent-teacher conference more authentic. Perhaps parents would be more willing to attend if they trusted that they would not get blindsided when they attended the conference.

A friend from high school commented on her private Facebook page that she wished she had the new Common Core report card before the conference so she didn't have to read it, digest the information, and

(Continued)

(Continued)

come up with a couple of questions in the 15-minute conference. After I read the comment (she's not a parent in my district), I contacted the other two elementary principals and they agreed to distribute the CCSS report cards in our district.

Parent-Teacher Discussion

Parent-teacher conferences are pretty intimidating to parents. They are walking into a situation where they may or may not know their child's teacher very well. It may be the first parent-teacher conference they have ever attended, depending on the grade of their child. Some conferences focus on *one to grow on, one to go on, and one to glow on* . . . while other conferences unfortunately focus more on what children can't do rather than what they can.

One way to hold a conference with a parent is to use their child as the facilitator. Student-led conferences, which you can read more about here, are a great way to make sure that the conference is child centered. Students get the opportunity to show their parents all the growth they have made over the quarter or trimester. Student-led conferences end with a teacher discussion about where the child is presently. Although they are a lot of work to set up, they're such a great way to have the students involved in a meeting that is about them.

Parent-teacher conferences should not be a surprise for parents. In this day and age of technology and enhanced communication tools, most parents should attend a meeting where they are not blindsided with bad news about their children. Unfortunately, with our present accountability system that focuses on numbers more than social-emotional learning, conferences are at risk of focusing on student weaknesses instead of student strengths.

Flipping parent conferences by sending home the report card before the conference rather than handing it to the parents at the conference is a great way to provide the parents with information that they can absorb, garner questions, and come to a meeting prepared to have authentic dialogue with their child's teacher.

Too often parent-teacher conferences are more about who controlled the conversation instead of providing everyone with the ability to come prepared to have a proper place at the table. Sure, there will are times when the report card is lost, the parent comes unprepared, or a parent cancels or doesn't show up, but I would venture to guess that when we treat parents as if they are going to do the right thing instead of assuming they will do the wrong thing, many parents rise to the challenge.

Source: http://blogs.edweek.org/edweek/finding_common_ground/2013/12/flipping_parent_conferences.html

By taking some very simple steps and sending out information ahead of time, we were able to enhance the conversation that parents were having with teachers, and in some cases those conversations involved students.

IN THE END

Flipping leadership can happen in every facet of what we do. The common idea is to flip faculty meetings, but a few initiatives and one bad parent meeting taught me to open up our virtual walls to parents. We no longer needed to control all of the information and provide it to them before they had a chance to digest what we said. Parents found new and innovative ways to be a part of our school dialogue. It wasn't always easy, and it isn't perfect. There will always be parents who do not watch the video, or perhaps they say something negative about it as they roll their eyes. However, there are so many other parents who appreciate the new form of communication, and we can no longer say that parents don't want to be involved in their child's learning. We must use innovative ways to show parents and the community that we want them to partner with us, and engage with them in ways that show that schooling has changed to meet the needs of their 21st century children.

ACTION STEPS

- Ensure that you have current e-mail information for parents.
- Invest in a parent portal that gives you the ability to e-mail as many parents as possible.
- Find a software application that you are comfortable with and can use to flip communication.
- Clearly articulate with parents what flipped communication means.
- Make sure parents understand that flipped communication will not replace newsletters.
- Try your best to shorten newsletters so they fit on a refrigerator. We named our newsletter *The Refrigerator Page.*

How to Flip
Communication

I hope that I provided you with a multitude of reasons to convince you to flip your faculty meetings and parent communication. It's important to remember that technology is a tool. Most connected educators agree with that. It's equally important to remember that flipped leadership involves using technology in various natural ways. It is not about creating artificial situations where leaders flip something and then weave it into what they are doing in order to prove its worthiness. As I mentioned earlier in this book, I did not use a lot of technology in my teaching career because it wasn't readily available. I only began to use it when I realized it could enhance my leadership at the same time as it made my life easier. With increased mandates and accountability, most school leaders saw the required number of formal observations also increase. Tenured teachers who were once allowed to perform goal setting for their Annual Professional Performance Review (APPR) are now required twice a year to be formally observed by their school leader. This, of and by itself, is not an issue, because school leaders should be in classrooms observing learning through teacher observations. It is the sheer number of observations that increased which poses a problem for all school leaders, which is why my recommendation to use an iPad and complete observations on a tablet becomes important. It makes life easier and happens to model appropriate technology behavior to students and staff at the same time.

For instance, as one event led to another, I found myself delving into flipped leadership, which for all intents and purposes happened by accident. When I took leadership courses and began my principalship, technology was not my first priority. I still consider myself a technology novice because I can't name numerous apps, organizational tools (i.e., Evernote, etc.), or examples of different cloud technologies. My approach is simple; I set a goal, and then find the best tools that can help me achieve those goals. It is fair to say that this approach has been accompanied by many mistakes. Colleagues have talked me through the use of DropBox and Google Plus, to name just a few tools. The important element to remember is that I didn't give up because I recognized the value in the technology tools.

In all honesty, I come from the Todd Whitaker school of thought, where I don't reinvent the wheel, and look for practical ways to get the job done. Sometimes those methods are innovative and other times they're old school. As much as I keep a calendar on my phone through Google, I keep a paper copy as well because I like to have a backup. Nevertheless, over the past two years the one area that I significantly trust is the impact flipped leadership can have on a school community. It's not because I created the idea; I just took the flipped classroom experience and brought it into the leadership realm. I trust flipped leadership because of the multitude of new connections I've made with staff, parents in our school community, and other educators.

IT'S WHAT YOU MAKE OF IT

If you approach flipped leadership as though it is a passing fad, that's exactly what it will be. Without a doubt, your school community can tell when you don't put your full attention into what you are doing. The important point to remember is that flipped leadership is what you make of it. There is no one-size-fits-all approach. There is enough of that conformity in education. Flipped leadership encourages creativity. Before a faculty meeting, leaders can send out articles or Ted Talks videos that focus on a goal set by the school stakeholder group and then discuss the article or video at the meeting. The point is to go deeper into our learning. Often, leaders and teachers try to do so many tasks at the same time that their communications only get to the surface level, and as educators, we need more than that. We need to take ideas and look at them from all sides. We need honest and respectful discourse so we can get the best out of our learning and inspire students to get the best out of their learning.

HOW TO FLIP YOUR LEADERSHIP

Start somewhere. I know that sounds like simple advice, but figure out which flipped experience you want to start with first. If it's for a faculty meeting, ensure that you prepare teachers by discussing why you are flipping the meeting. One of my best flipped faculty meetings focused on evidence-based observations. I provided a link to an article and video prior to the meeting, and then met with faculty to discuss what I look for when I walk into a teacher observation. In return, teachers articulated what they wanted me to see, and then we watched the video together. The teachers had to write down what they saw on the video and explain where they thought the teacher performed well and where she could improve. In this example, the video (which I would probably not use again) focused more on the teacher, therefore we really didn't focus on student learning. In the future, I intend to locate a better video to illustrate student learning over teacher instruction.

If you decide to focus on flipping parent communication, find a place to start. I would suggest sending a video out before your next Parent Teacher Association (PTA, national) and Parent Teacher Organization (PTO, private) meeting. For example, if you are preparing for an upcoming science fair, you can send out a flipped video using pictures that show the best examples of what students can do at a science fair. Another idea, which was also an example of the best flipped communication I did with parents in my school community, is to send out information regarding the Common Core State Standards before Open House. I find that the Common Core State Standards (CCSS) are misunderstood in many states due to poor implementation, and flipping the information and then discussing it at Open House can be a great way to weed through the issues as well as the positives of this important topic. I simply grab my iPad and click on the TouchCast app.

HOW I DO IT

Follow the directions and move on. There are many different resources to use to create flipped videos. I find TouchCast to be very user-friendly. In the past, I created a Prezi (cloud-based software that designs and creates presentations) and then recorded it on Screenr, a web-based screen recorder, but Screenr is a paid service for videos over five minutes long, and it is best to keep your videos under 5 minutes. In addition, another disadvantage is that Screenr has an automatic repayment policy every year, and they do not send out an e-mail prior to charging your credit card. TouchCast is free and available on iPads and any desktop or laptop.

As you become more familiar with the process you can incorporate different pictures, short videos within your video, and music. Just be careful not to make it so creative that the message gets lost. Flipping leadership is about delivering a message in a way that describes the intended meeting and informs, encourages, and triggers deeper interest and conversation on the part of the recipient when you meet in person.

IN THE END

Flipping leadership is about enhancing a leader's communication with all stakeholders in her or his school community. In my own practices, I upload the videos I sent out to my YouTube channel, and then I have a record of when parents, students, and teachers are viewing them more than once. In a time when the dialogue about school has been more of a monologue about how we are failing, flipping my leadership has helped promote the school and connect with parents who cannot always make it to school events. In addition, it has helped create a sense of pride with teachers, staff, and students because it focuses on the positive rather than the negative.

Now, go and flip something . . .

References

Bergmann, J., & Sams, A. (2012). *Flip your classroom: Reach every student in every class every day.* Eugene, OR: International Society for Technology in Education (ISTE).

Covey, S. R. (1989). *The 7 habits of highly effective people.* New York: Simon & Schuster.

DeWitt, P. (2011a, November 1). Student-led conferences [Web blog post]. *Education Week, Finding Common Ground.* Retrieved from http://blogs.edweek.org/edweek/finding_common_ground/2011/11/student-led_conferences.html

DeWitt, P. (2011b, November 21). Why educators should join Twitter [Web blog post]. *Education Week, Finding Common Ground.* Retrieved from http://blogs.edweek.org/edweek/finding_common_ground/2011/11/why_educators_should_join_twitter.html

DeWitt, P. (2012a). *Dignity for all: Safeguarding LGBT students.* Thousand Oaks, CA: Corwin.

DeWitt, P. (2012b, August 15). A new approach to teaching? The flipped classroom [Web blog post]. *Education Week, Finding Common Ground.* Retrieved from http://blogs.edweek.org/edweek/finding_common_ground/2012/08/a_new_approach_to_teaching_the_flipped_classroom.html

DeWitt, P. (2012c, September 2). The flipped faculty meeting [Web blog post]. *Education Week, Finding Common Ground.* Retrieved from http://blogs.edweek.org/edweek/finding_common_ground/2012/09/the_flipped_faculty_meeting.html

DeWitt, P. (2013, December 6). Flipping parent conferences? [Web blog post]. *Education Week, Finding Common Ground.* Retrieved from http://blogs.edweek.org/edweek/finding_common_ground/2013/12/flipping_parent_conferences.html

DeWitt, P. (2014, January 9). I hate technology and other lame opinions [Web blog post]. *Education Week, Finding Common Ground.* Retrieved from http://blogs.edweek.org/edweek/finding_common_ground/2014/01/i_hate_technology_and_other_lame_opinions.html

Ferlazzo, L. (2012, August 11). *The best posts on the "flipped classroom" idea* [Web blog post]. Retrieved from http://larryferlazzo.edublogs.org/2012/08/11/the-best-posts-on-the-flipped-classroom-idea/

Hattie, J. (2009). *Visible learning: A synthesis of over 800 meta-analyses relating to achievement.* London, UK: Routledge.

Hattie, J. (2012). *Visible learning for teachers: Maximizing impact on learning.* London, UK: Routledge.

Pierce-Picciotto, L. (1996). *Student-led parent conferences.* New York: Scholastic.

Robinson, K. (2006). How schools kill creativity [Web video file]. *Ted Talks.* Retrieved from http://www.ted.com/talks/ken_robinson_says_schools_kill_creativity

Sheninger, E. (2014). *Digital leadership: Changing paradigms for changing times.* Thousand Oaks, CA: Corwin.

CORWIN
A SAGE Company

The Corwin logo—a raven striding across an open book—represents the union of courage and learning. Corwin is committed to improving education for all learners by publishing books and other professional development resources for those serving the field of PreK–12 education. By providing practical, hands-on materials, Corwin continues to carry out the promise of its motto: **"Helping Educators Do Their Work Better."**